HOW TO DEAL WITH THE SILENT TREATMENT

Cheryl T. Long

Copyright @ 2020 by Cheryl T. Long

All rights reserved. No part of this publication may be reproduced, distributed, or transmitted in any form or by any means, including photocopying, recording, or other electronic or mechanical methods, without the prior written permission of the publisher, except in the case of brief quotations embodied in critical reviews and certain other noncommercial uses permitted by copyright law. Portions of this book are works of nonfiction. Certain names and identifying characteristics have been changed

Ordering Information:

Quantity sales. Special discounts are available on quantity purchases by corporations, associations, and others. For details, contact me at

www.deardaughterslovesmom.com

Printed in the United States of America

Dedication

This book is dedicated to "Self-Love" because "Self-Love" is the greatest love of all!!!

Acknowledgments

First and foremost I would like to thank God. In the course of putting this book together, I appreciated how true this gift of writing is for me. You've given me the power to believe in my passion and follow my dreams. I could never have done this without the faith I have in you, the Almighty.

To my Mom and Dad Elizabeth and Kenneth: "For the first time in 40 years, I am speechless! I can barely find the words to express all the wisdom, love and support you've given me. You are my #1fans, and for that, I am eternally grateful."

To my children, Devon, Anjanae, Shinera and Robyn: "You are the best thing that I have ever done in my life! You welcomed me into motherhood, and I am so grateful for all of you. Mommy loves you more than you will ever know and my writing is proof of the beauty I see whenever I look into your eyes, know this!"

Table of Contents

Introduction 1

The "Silent Treatment": One of the Most Lethal Weapons of the Narcissistic Arsenal 3

The "Silent Treatment" is a Demonstration of Power. That's It. 5

There are several types of "Silent Treatment" 7

Some sequels of the "Silent Treatment" 9

How to react to "Silent Treatment" 12

How to Treat Silent Processing in a Relationship . 15

Silent Treatment Abuse: How to Take a Position and Regain Control 18

6 Ways to Combat the Silent Abuse Treatment 20

How to Handle Silent Processing 26

ADHD Relations: Dealing with Silent Treatment . 37

In Conclusion 41

About Author 43

More Books by the Author: 44

Introduction

There are things that you absolutely must say during the time of conflict with your partner, and there are things that you shouldn't say. But what if your partner's conflict style is to say nothing at all? Whether the reason you are fighting is as commonplace as a missed date or as serious as cheating, the silent treatment is a major obstacle to overcoming a relational struggle.

Generally, people are silent when they are too angry, and they do not want to communicate until they have had time to recollect, deal with their emotions, and then discuss from a place of love. People also use silent processing as a passive, and aggressive way to manipulate someone to accept their conditions.

Getting the silent treatment of a partner or friend is not fun; Concepción explains it as a form of manipulation or emotional coercion. In addition, silent processing is a mechanism that is used when someone wants to avoid confrontation with someone else. While doing this, a fight would be delayed, and it is confrontation that advances relationships.

The "Silent Treatment": One of the Most Lethal Weapons of the Narcissistic Arsenal

The "Silent Treatment" is one of the most used and most lethal strategies of the narcissistic predator. It refrains all communication with the victim, accompanying this gesture with a cold and distant attitude. It removes the "word" from the person, ignoring it completely, as if it does not exist or it was not there.

Frequently, this behavior is first displayed by the narcissist, without being preceded by any discussion or disagreement that could explain it. Perhaps in his deranged mind, it is a way to punish the victim for some comment made, which he considers as criticism on the part of the person. He would never directly say the reason for his behavior, so the victim cannot understand the cause of his action therefore generating deep anxiety and anguish on the victim's part.

Whether there is a "reason" or not, I am convinced that the main reason why the narcissist applies the "Silent Treatment" is to obtain minimum expenditure of energy, and the power of negative fuel to which he is addicted to. Frustration, anger, fear, anxiety, confusion, anguish, bewilderment and so on are emotional vampires that feed on the problem created by people who relate with them. The "Silent Treatment" empowers them by making them feel like the bosses or in control; it also reaffirms their superiority.

The "Silent Treatment" is a Demonstration of Power. That's It.

Through these manipulative tactics, the narcissist plays with the feelings of the other person; the fear of definitive abandonment on the part of the other person demonstrates that he can easily dispense with it.

I'll say from now on that the "Silent Treatment" is an ABUSE in every rule — ABUSE with a capital letter, and a red-red flag to identify the narcissist. It is not a trait of character, nor a change of mood of the abuser; he deliberately applies it to some people (not to others), which shows that he knows exactly what he is doing, and he has a purpose in his perverse agenda.

The silence of the narcissist is always significant; it transmits contempt, indicates cold fury, and seeks to indoctrinate the victim to be more submissive. It also punishes and warns the victim about the consequences of her actions, therefore demonstrating the narcissist's lack of empathy, disdain, and indifference for the victim's feelings and emotions.

There are several types of "Silent Treatment"

A. "Silent treatment" Present: It is exercised while the victim is present. Its duration is usually short, a few hours or sometimes a day. The narcissist shows an impassive expression, a glacial mask, responding by giving the "cold shoulder" (Cold Shoulder).

B. "Silent Treatment" Absent: It is applied in the absence of the victim, the narcissist disappears without a trace for several days or weeks and does not answer calls or reply text messages. There is no prior explanation or warning before communication stops. In addition to extracting fuel, it is also a way to punish the victim and show how easy it is to get rid of the victim.

C. "Silent treatment" Thematic: The narcissist stops talking about certain personal issues with his victim, the conversation is limited to common and inconsequential matters. All this makes the couple to understand that there is a decrease in trust level. The narcissist is cold and extremely reserved, does not explain his absences, keeps his affairs secret, therefore making the other person feel like a stranger. This subtle form of silence is a way of devaluing the victim and separating her from the circle of her interests. This discomfort is exacerbated in the presence of the third parties; the predator is open and jovial, which contrasts the attitude that he maintains with the victim, even in the presence of witnesses.

Some sequels of the "Silent Treatment"

The "Silent Treatment" is a tremendously destructive manipulation tactic. It directly attacks the most basic needs of human beings: attention and affection, especially on the part of those who claim to "love us." That's why it's so cruel. We all need our existence to be recognized; when we are ignored in this way, we are completely denigrated. This is why its consequences are lethal for the psychic and emotional life of those who suffer from it.

For a reason that is best known, some people refer to "Silent Treatment" as a silent or psychological murder, and its impact may even be greater than an act of physical violence.

We should never allow anyone, under any excuse, apply this weapon of emotional destruction to our self-esteem. And much less a person who professes to love us as a friend, partner, etc. At the first sign they are subjecting us to "Silent Treatment," we should react by putting ourselves psychologically safe and not let them destroy us nor manipulate us in that way.

If a couple or friend tries to apply the "law of silence" and we "take the word" right away, it is a clear sign of the degree of toxicity of that person. Let's not forget it's an abuse, and nothing else. In a healthy relationship, there can be moments of tension and moments of withdrawal from communication to avoid further conflicts and misunderstandings, but it is important to know how to differentiate them from the manipulative and sadistic behavior of the emotional predator.

In a healthy relationship, these silences are a truce that aims to perhaps relieve tensions and resume communication in a more propitious climate.

The "Silent Treatment" I'm talking about in this book does not seek the reflection of the parties, nor does it intend to clarify or offer explanations of any kind. It does not consider neither is it respectful of the other person's feelings, rather, it is manipulative, abusive, and full of empowerment (of the narcissist) in its purest form.

How to react to "Silent Treatment"

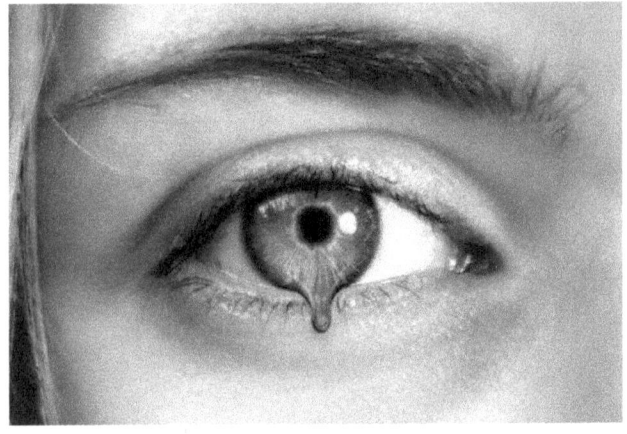

When the narcissist submits his victim to "Silent Treatment," what he wants is for his victim to run after him and beg him to talk to her again; to cry and express her anguish and even to blame herself for having displeased his executioner. If none of this happens, and the victim does not react, he would act as if the matter doesn't concern her, and the narcissist would remain disarmed.

In fact, the only indicated response to the "Silent Treatment" is NOT TO REACT. It might be difficult but there is no other formula to make his manipulation strategy ineffective. The treatment will be ineffective if you immerse yourself in your silence while he is present, then withdraw from the site ipso facto without fuss, allegations or emotional expression. His evil game works if we are at his side: if we leave immediately and he remains alone, the stars will be the ones that will tolerate his toxic silence.

We are not obliged, under any circumstance, to remain by the side of a person who submits us to this type of perverse game.

Abstain from claims; do not ask for explanations, or try to make him see the toxicity and damage his behavior puts on you — it is useless because it will only create an opportunity for him to further manipulate you. Let's just continue with our lives as though it was nothing, and if he returns to talk to us, don't not have a party, just act as if nothing had happened. In this way, you bring down his attempt to extract fuel through this insidious manipulative tactic. No "narcissistic supply," neither positive nor negative. Nothing is nothing.

I am aware that it is easier to write it than to do it, but it is the only way to deactivate this destructive bomb that is the "Silent Treatment."

If the "Silent Treatment" is the absent type, take advantage of his absence to free yourself of the toxicity, so we can take care of our life. When the victim fails to seek the narcissist, the narcissist would be curious to know why. For him, that means he is no longer in control as he believed, and sooner or later he will return to try to retake his power over you.

In short, our biggest weapon against "Silent Treatment" is simply to ignore and restrain from reacting, thereby, leaving it without effect. Leaving the situation unattended to is the narcissist's fear; they become wounded in their inflated pride, which causes them to retire and look for fuel elsewhere. Whatever mode/type of silent treatment the narcissist adopts, do not get overwhelmed, neither should you seek explanations that do not exist but be indifferent with no worries, anguish or reaction — just let everything sink into its toxic silence for centuries to come.

How to Treat Silent Processing in a Relationship

There are things you absolutely must say during a time of conflict with your partner and there are things that you totally should not say. But what if your partner's conflict style is to say nothing at all? Whether the reason you are fighting is as commonplace as a missed date or as serious as cheating, the silent treatment is a major obstacle to overcoming a relational struggle. In this book are some tactics you can adopt to handle such situations.

Generally, people are silent when they are too angry and they do not want to communicate until they have time to recollect, deal with their emotions, and to discuss from a place of love. People also use silent processing as a passive, aggressive way of manipulating someone to accept their conditions.

Getting the silent treatment from a partner or friend is not fun; Concepción explains it as a form of manipulation or emotional coercion. In addition, silent processing is a mechanism used when someone wants to avoid confrontation with someone else. While doing this, a fight can be delayed, and it is confrontation that advances relationships.

For these reasons, it might be tempting to react aggressively to silent processing. However, Concepción recommends starting with a different approach — empathy. By approaching your friend/partner with this, you send a message that your relationship is more important than the problem in question. The best way to deal with this is from a place of worry. Asking someone why they seem a little quiet is a non-confrontational way to engage them; it also shows them that you are too much in love to tolerate any passive aggression and unrepressed resentment.

If your friend or partner does not respond to kindness, Concepción says the next step is to be honest with them. Sometimes, being direct will push that person to talk about his/her feelings, so that you can work towards a solution. We teach people how to treat us; so when someone gives the silent treatment, let them know that you are informed about what they are trying to do, and it is not allowed.

As a last resort, just ask your friend or whoever it is when he/she is ready to talk to you again. In the meantime, Concepción recommends to do the only thing you can do in these types of situations: concentrate on your own happiness.

Silent Treatment Abuse: How to Take a Position and Regain Control

Abuse of silent treatment is an abuse like in any other relationship. It is a way to control and incite a reaction from you, bringing out the worst in you. Just to be clear, giving someone silent treatment is the "abuse of silent treatment." It is simply a way to control and manipulate someone by not talking to them without giving them a cause. The silent treatment makes you know when someone is angry with you, but they will not tell you why. Worse, they will not even tell you they're crazy; they just ignore you.

This leaves you with your mind, and it drives you crazy. Nothing is worse than trying to get something out of someone that does not want to give it. If your partner does not respond to you, then there is nothing you can do about it; making attempts to make your partner talk only makes you more miserable.

Why silent treatment is the worst abuse

I do not know who has the license for it, but the silent treatment is the worst form of abuse that will make someone criticize you. There is nothing worse than the feeling of "you have done something wrong, but not being able to get answers from the person you think you wronged."

If you receive the answer: "nothing" or "good" followed by days, weeks, or even months of silence, it is a form of abuse designed to control you and make the other person feel an inch taller.

6 Ways to Combat the Silent Abuse Treatment

The abuse of silent treatment is the key feature of a narcissist — I'm not saying you're with a narcissist, I do not know you, or the person who does it to you. What I do know is that the classic sign of narcissism is when someone gets you to do what they want by retaining the love and attention they had been giving you. They hold back communication and information about what you have done for so long. It positions you to do whatever you can to obtain the punishment of the silence rose once and for all.

When you get into an argument with someone, you usually have a "cooling period." It is a moment when you both decide not to get into each other for a day or two. A waiting time for communication allows both of them to heal, but the silent treatment is very different.

In the abuse of silent treatment, one partner continually approaches the other but is always being ignored and punished. If you are the recipient of the abuse of silent treatment, it not only ruins your relationship; it destroys the days and weeks of your life. To stop the abuse, you have to regain control and try to divert the ways in which the abuse comes your way.

How to stop someone who is using the abuse of silent treatment on you

1. Ignore: If you want someone to stop using the abuse of silent treatment, stop informing them that it bothers you. Like someone who is intimidating you, if you ignore them and they do not get an uproar from you, then they will give up and stop the behavior.

The silent treatment is a tactic to manipulate and control you. If you show them that you cannot be manipulated, then they will stop wasting their energy on you or give something else a try. And who knows, they may give up completely and probably grow up.

So, how do you ignore it? Stop asking what is wrong or trying to find ways to communicate: watch TV, invite a friend to dinner, just do whatever you need to get distracted from what they are doing to you. Pretend to be completely oblivious to what they do, so that they can stop wasting their time and energy.

2. Face it with a smile: If you agree with yourself that you're still happy, then they are not bringing you down, making you desperate, or guiding your mood. If you want them to stop treating you with abuse of silent treatment, simply continue your day with a smile and an uplifted spirit.

I KNOW, I really know. I have been there. It is one of the most difficult things that can be done in the world, especially if you are an empathetic person and they are people that you love. But the only way to stop them from cussing and controlling you is to do your job, be happy and smiling, as if you are not careful in the world. This sends the message that you do not care if they try to manipulate you; it will not work.

3. Do not give what you're given in return: If you think that the silent treatment can be stopped in the same way, you are absolutely wrong. It will only make the situation worse. It is natural to give in return what you are given and stop talking to them, but it will not solve the problem.

If you keep silent right away, then you are like

them. Do not use the silent treatment, just talk to them like you would do on any other day. You cannot beat them by joining them, so do not silence them again.

4. Do not give up when you approach them: Whatever you do, try not to force a conversation with them. The only way to break the abuse is to be sure that if they do not talk to you, you are fine without them and will survive.

The best way to stop the desperation of trying to reach them is to think about all the other times they gave you the silent treatment and how you survived. Instead of taking them out of their ridiculousness (if they do not respond), go on with your day as you would with any other. Do not give up but do not manipulate yourself either, else, you will do it forever.

5. Do not play into their hands: If you attack them with anger, resentment, or sarcasm, then you are doing exactly what they want you to do. Look, the reason they are silent is because they want you to lose your shit and fly out in frustration and fear.

When you do it, they return it to you. What happens when you persecute them and say things out of anger and frustration during the silent treatment? You will probably end up feeling bad and sorry; that's where they want you. It is in your reaction and behavior that they find their control. Do not play with that.

If they do not speak, leave them. Do not play in their hands to give them what they want. If you behave badly, you will feel bad about it. You will not survive with the respect for yourself.

6. Leave the relationship and find happiness: If everything fails, stop the cycle and save yourself. Make no mistake; abuse of silent treatment is abuse. If you ever hear someone say that they are "closing," that is another term for the abuse of silent treatment.

Either because they do not know what to say or even how they feel, it is not your responsibility to make them grow and speak.

The more you try to take advantage of it, the worse it will be for you. The silent treatment is a control mechanism to create a reaction, feel remorse for reacting, and start feeling bad for yourself. Then, stop feeding him. If you cannot make it stop, then, for your own good, you may have to move forward.

If you understand this, you know the desperation you feel; it is not worth it. It is worthwhile to be in a relationship with an adult who will talk about their problems, not keep you hostage with the abuse of silent treatment.

How to Handle Silent Processing

Have you ever had a disagreement with a loved one and you end up with tight and terse answers, or a lack of response? If so, you may have received the silent treatment. Also known as the "cold shoulder," people sometimes use the silent treatment as a way to get away from an argument while considering their options, or as a means of retaliation. Being the recipient of silent processing can make you feel invisible and manipulated. Take back your power in this situation by adopting healthier communication styles, working on yourself rather than becoming obsessed with the other person, and identifying and ending emotional abuse.

Method 1

Break this communication model:

Refrain from showing a reaction. Although some people engage in a silent treatment without realizing its toxic effects on relationships, some people withdraw voluntarily and are unaware that they are hurting the other's feelings. In any case, if you start to apologize (and you do not even know what you did wrong) or if you start begging the person to pay attention to you, you are feeding the beast.

- Instead, take a silent treatment as a green light to gather yourself. Do not show anger, neither should you aggressively force the person to talk to you. Do not provoke an argument, but give them and yourself a little space until things calm down.

- When you are around the person, strive to appear relaxed and positive. Do not suggest or say to the person how his/her behavior has affected you negatively, even if it does.

Ask for a time to discuss the question. People

who practice silent processing essentially send signals indicating what they need because they are not able to effectively communicate what their needs are. Your friend or a partner may not be trying to hurt you by moving away; on the contrary, they are probably trying to heal their own wounds after a fight. Take the high road and do what they are not able to do: choose a time to discuss the issue as adults.

- Say: "We are both emotional and need time to think. Why don't we give it a few hours and come back around 3 pm to end this discussion? "

- This prevents silent processing from having an impact because silence is agreed upon. Then, once you have both gained some objectivity, try to solve the misunderstanding.

See things from the positive side: keep in mind that communication is a give and take. If your loved ones are trying to avoid you or block communication, never react back in the same way, just try and see the thing from a positive side.

- Review the exchange that preceded the silent treatment and consider what the other person said. What did you say in return? If you put yourself in their place, how would you feel?

- For example, consider that you pressured your mother to let you go to a party, so she started ignoring you. Reflecting from her point of view, you realize that it is frustrating to be under pressure and that you would be bored too.

- If you still feel embarrassed by the person's silence, try talking to a friend or trusted member to get an outside perspective of the situation. Make sure you talk to someone who will be honest and kind to you.

Use the "I" statements when the discussion takes place. The silent treatment is a passive-aggressive approach that can also trigger passive aggression in you. The other person refuses to share their feelings or engage in a conversation, so you have decided to ignore them immediately. Instead, use an assertive approach that can help you get your message across without making the situation worse.

- "I" statements are convenient ways to share your thoughts and feelings without blaming the other person. You could say, "When I'm ignored, I feel small and helpless. I wish we could be more active in sharing our feelings and not withdrawing from each other. Next time, can you ask for space instead of ignoring me?"

- When you are speaking with the person, be sure to set an example and react with kindness, humility, respect, and self-control. Avoid accusing the person of things or assuming his intentions.

Method 2

Focus on yourself:

Identify your role in the silent processing cycle. Once you have some space, you can use that time to think about how you played a role in the silence of the other person. This does not put you in default but gives you the power to recognize and change any type of communication that may lead you at this stage.

- As you reflect on your interactions with the person, try to find common patterns in your own behavior. For example, your boyfriend was talking and you interrupted him because you thought you knew what he was going to say. Silent treatment can be followed soon after. Your tendency to "predict" thoughts can be a source of frustration that drives him away.

- You can minimize your role in silent processing in this scenario by practicing active listening. Do not interfere with your partner when he speaks. Give them time to fully express their message before responding.

Reduce anger so as not to make the situation worse. Feeling manipulated can generate anger within you, it can push an already useless interaction into dangerous territory. Recognize that it does not help if your relationship always displays anger. Use the space you have during the silent treatment to minimize the negative emotions you feel.

- Try relaxation techniques such as guided imagery, deep breathing, progressive muscle relaxation, or gentle stretching to reduce anger and ensure calmness.

- If you need time to calm down, try taking a one-hour break or even agree to postpone the conversation until the next day, but do not delay it too long.

Set personal boundaries. When you effectively

define the boundaries of your relationships, you increase the chances of living according to your values. Whether the person giving the silent treatment is a parent, a best friend, or a lover, you can limit your own feelings of hurt by this toxic relational schema by developing personal boundaries.

- Set boundaries by thinking first about how you want to be treated in your relationships and what you will accept and reject from those who are around you. Once these boundaries are established, share these expectations with your loved ones. Keep in mind that if you have been abused in the past, you may feel confused about how you should be treated in your relationships. First, try to talk about your situation with a trusted friend.

- For example, you could say, "I want you and love spending time with you. But when you suddenly stop talking to me, it makes me confused and helpless. If you continue to do this, I will have to distance myself from you to protect my own emotional health and well-being."

Perform personal care. Regardless of whether

the person wants to hurt you or not, receiving silent treatment is not good. Spend time doing things that relax you and make you smile so as to counter the negative effects of the silent treatment.

- Exercise. Call a trusted friend. Visit a local park or a museum. Light a candle and take a bubble bath. These are all great ideas for treating yourself to improve your mental health during the silent treatment.

Method 3:

Dealing with psychological violence

Notice the link between silent treatment and narcissism. If silent treatment is a chronic behavioral style of your loved one, this person may have narcissistic traits. Narcissism is frequently used to describe the personality disorder in a person who naturally exploits and manipulates those around him to his advantage.

- If you find yourself constantly apologizing for the things you did not do or begging your partner to contact you, he might use your answer to gain the upper hand in the relationship.

- Being in touch with a narcissist can be exhausting and confusing. However, you can implement some strategies to improve your interactions with this person. Individual therapy can also help you to learn to manage their behavior.

Develop better communication skills in a therapy. If you want to become a better communicator (and your loved one is also interested), using professional advisors can help you. You can do individual consultation, as a couple or even as a family. Whether you are dealing with a family member or your spouse, participating in therapy helps you to identify the roles that both parties play in the silent treatment, therefore breaking the cycle of emotional abuse.

- For example, participating in therapy can help you recognize healthier ways to express your requests, for example by using "I" statements, sandwich criticism, or asking for a specific time to discuss grievances.

- On the other hand, it can teach your loved one how to be more verbal about their thoughts and feelings and how to handle their frustration more effectively than the stone wall.

Surround yourself with people who

communicate in a healthy way: If you are a frequent victim of the silent treatment, this relationship pattern can be detrimental to your health and well-being. In order to work on your health, it is essential to spend time with people who communicate in a healthy way.

- Contact friends and loved ones who support you and value your personality. Just say, "My relationship has been rather difficult. I could use a little time with a friend. Do you want to go out this weekend?"

- Another option is to participate in a support group for those who have been victims of narcissistic abuse. You can ask your therapist for a referral or look for support groups online.

Quit the relationship with an emotional abuser who refuses to change. The silent treatment is one of the many tactics employed by the emotional abuser. One partner feels intimidated and helpless towards the other. If you have tried to improve your communication with your loved one and he/she refuses to recognize his/her share in the silent treatment, you may need to be separate.

- You could tell your loved one, "I cannot be in this relationship anymore because I feel controlled and helpless. I tried to work with you on this issue, but you totally refused. I have to do what is best for me. "

- Practice what you will say with a friend or therapist. This can help you feel more confident about breaking up with an emotional abuser.

ADHD Relations: Dealing with Silent Treatment

When you go out with someone with ADHD, romance and mystery can last longer than you think.

It is a fact that the mystery of romance fades away after a while. Well, when you go out with someone with ADHD, it can last longer than you think. It can be a good thing to enjoy the endless creativity and spontaneity of people with the ADHD brain type, which includes about 15 million Americans according to the CDC.

Then, there is the wrong kind of mystery. After the honeymoon period, just at the time of the first or second true argument in the relationship, things can change quickly. To put it plainly, there may come a time when your partner with ADHD simply stops talking. This can be painful and confusing, and no matter what you try, you will probably have no chance to draw an explanation for your loved one. The relationship will just implode.

So, what's really going on? Believe it or not, it's a pretty predictable cycle of communication. To understand it, you need to step back and consider the whole life experience of living with ADHD. Since kindergarten, this person has been scolded, shouted at, punished, and mocked just for doing things that seemed natural to him. He never understood what was happening, why the behavior was bad, or why he was different from other children. Most ADHD were simply slapped with labels such as "bad," "hyper," or "silly," and knew by heart the path that led them to the principal's office.

Explode yourself with a few decades, and these scars are deep. Whenever a person whom the ADHD cares about expresses anger or frustration, he reacts excessively. Mentally, they go back to primary school, feel confused and embarrassed as they are being punished again. Instead of dealing with relationship problems through healthy, open discussions, the ADHD will go into self-protection, essentially killing people. They know from the experience that a relationship starts to spoil, and that's when they choose to stop.

It should also be noted that this mode of communication during a confrontation is not unique to men or people with ADHD, it is found commonly in people who have been repeatedly disciplined or publicly humiliated while growing up. To overcome this obstacle in a relationship, communication patterns must change. You will have to work together, and the non-ADHD partner in particular should try to be understanding and patient. Follow these steps:

- The non-ADHD partner should put himself in the ADHD partner's place. You have to understand that this happens because of a painful pattern of one's personal story. This may seem counter-intuitive, but this behavior is not for you personally.

- The non-ADHD partner must resist the urge to make assumptions about what the ADHD partner thinks. It is very frustrating that he or she stopped talking with you, but do not put the words in his mouth. Your imagination will go to the worst conclusions, which is not right for you, and this will make the disagreement much tenser.

- Recognize the situation for what it is. Tell

your ADHD partner that you need to talk about your disagreement, but in a way that makes them feel safe. Let them know that no one is being punished or vilified. As calmly, and as neutral as possible, explain where your head is.

- Then, this step is very important as it explains what you think of your partner, and ask if you are right or wrong. Give your partner the chance to explain his side of things. He will be relieved to have a glimpse of your thoughts and correct any misconception.

- Once you have both given your honest opinion, find a way to compromise on the issue so that you both can get what you want. Then do something fun to celebrate the new beginning of a much healthier communication.

Once you get into the habit of explaining your motivations as soon as a confrontation begins, you will be surprised how easy it is to resolve disputes. Better still, your loved one will become his habitual and amazing human being again.

In Conclusion

For obvious reasons, it might be tempting to react aggressively to silent processing. However, Concepción recommends starting with a different approach: empathy. By approaching your friend/partner this way, you send a message that your relationship is more important than the problem in a question. The best way to deal with this is from a place of worry. Asking someone why they seem a little quiet is a non-confrontational way to engage them, it also shows them that you are too much in love to tolerate any passive aggression and unrepressed resentment.

If your friend or partner does not respond to kindness, Concepción says the next step is just, to be honest with them. Sometimes, being direct will push that person to talk about his feelings, so that you can work towards a solution. We teach people how to treat us; so when someone gives the silent treatment, let them know that you are informed about what they are trying to do and that it is not allowed.

As a last resort, just ask your friend (or whoever it is) when he is ready to talk to you again. In the meantime, Concepción recommends that the only thing to do in this type of situation is to concentrate on your own happiness.

About Author

Cheryl T. Long is a multi-talented author. A mother of 4 beautiful children and a medical office manager who loves to write and share her stories with all she come in contact with. She had one vision in her mind — to give people around her an imaginable outlet.

More Books by the Author:

Love Yourself (Breaking the chains of self doubt)

Facing the Fear on being Alone

How to Deal with the silent treatment

Toxic People who to deal with Them

Letting go of a toxic relationship

Letting Go and Letting God (Ways to surrender control)

Exchange Emotional Pain for Peace and Prosperity

All book available in print and E-book

Stay in touch

www.deardaughterslovesmom. com

www.ingramcontent.com/pod-product-compliance
Lightning Source LLC
Chambersburg PA
CBHW061301040426
42444CB00010B/2461